Term

Dane Joe

Presentation by *BookLeaf Publishing*

Web: www.bookleafpub.com

E-mail: info@bookleafpub.com

ISBN: 9789357690911

First edition 2022

1

1

Will any of this matter tomorrow?

2

My mind goes into overdrive at night.

3

A child's laughter is pure.

4

Let it go.

5

5

Maybe I think too much.

Social media is killing me gently and gradually.
I can't stop.

7

7

Maybe we can be a little kinder.

8

I should go outside more often and clear my head.

9

9

Do you think about it too?

10

I am re-living a happy memory.

11

11

I keep finding my own flaws in your perfection.

12

12

I want what they have.

13

I will do better next time.

14

14

I think my younger self would be surprised.

15

15

That meant a lot to me.

16

I don't know if I will ever tell you this.

17

I wonder who I will be in five years.

18

What if I didn't make that one specific decision on that one specific day?

19

19

I am trying to understand.

20

If I spoke to myself as I would a best friend, I would not say the same things.

21

I hate endings and goodbyes.

www.ingramcontent.com/pod-product-compliance
Lightning Source LLC
Chambersburg PA
CBHW070731160726
48003CB00006BA/2448